Royal Fireworks   Language Arts   by Michael Clay Thompson

BUILDING LANGUAGE

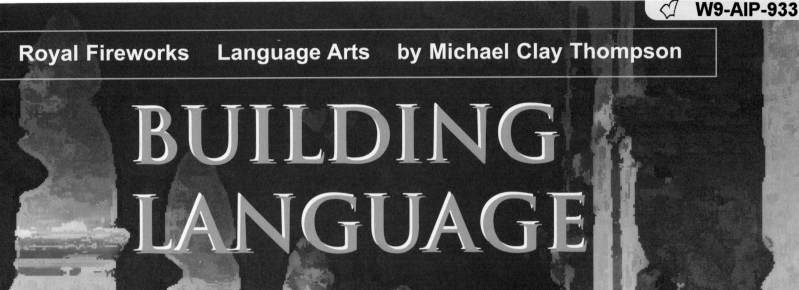

Michael Clay Thompson

Royal Fireworks Press

JULY 2012

Copyright @ 2003, Royal Fireworks Publishing Company, Inc.
All Rights Reserved — All Copying Prohibited
Royal Fireworks Publishing Company
First Avenue, P.O. Box 399
Unionville, NY 10988
845 726-4444
FAX 845 726-3824
Website: rfwp.com
Email: mail@rfwp.com
ISBN: **978-0-88092-906-6**
Printed in the United States of America
on acid-free paper using vegetable-based inks
by the Royal Fireworks Printing Company
of Unionville, New York.

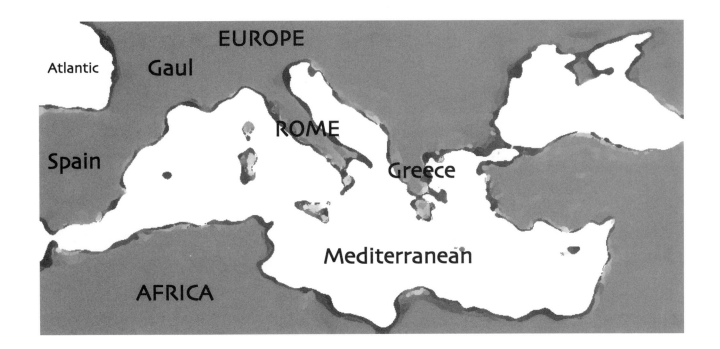

ROME, ROCKS, WORDS

Two thousand years ago,
before Europeans discovered
the back of the world and its people,
ancient Rome ruled the lands
surrounding the Mediterranean Sea.

Today the ruins of the
ancient capital of Rome are
in the modern city of Rome, Italy,
and the remains of the great buildings and roads
that the Romans built can be found
from England, to Africa, to Spain.

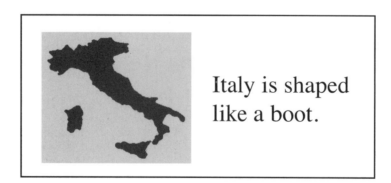

Italy is shaped
like a boot.

In these silent ruins, we still see
one of Rome's greatest gifts
to human civilization, the **arch**.

THE ARCH

The **arch**, with its graceful curve
of hand-shaped stones
gave Roman buildings
strength and beauty
and was important
to ancient construction.

At the center of the arch is the **keystone**,
shaped to send the weight and force
of the arch down to the ground below.

The arch shifts the weight
to the columns on either side.

AQUEDUCTS

Romans used rows of arches,
one on top of another,
to make **aqueducts**
which carried cold, fresh water
from the mountains down to the city.
In the aqueduct at Segovia, Spain,
there is no cement;
the arches are so strong
that the aqueduct still stands.

The Romans used the arch
to make strong bridges over rushing rivers.
With these bridges
Rome improved transportation
and connected the great empire together.

The Roman arch
was shaped like
a semicircle, a half-circle.

The Romans used rows of arches
to build the walls of great coliseums
where gladiators fought
in front of roaring crowds.

See how the arches are semicircles?

Some of the arches
the Romans built are huge.
They rise high in the air,
and support a massive weight of stone.

Arches allowed the Romans to build
great public buildings,
and the arch is so strong a form
that many of these buildings
are still standing,
almost 2,000 years
after the Roman Empire fell.

When the Romans
wanted to honor a hero,
they would sometimes build a
magnificent ornamental arch,
such as the one at right,
dedicated to Emperor Constantine,
who won a great battle in 315 A.D.

The head of a bust of Constantine.

Great Roman arches still inspire
modern architects.

The Roman-style arch in Washington Square,
which is in New York City's
Greenwich Village,
was built in 1889 to honor
the centennial of George Washington's
inauguration as President
of the United States.

ARCADE

A row of arches
is an **arcade**.
The Romans used
arcades in buildings,
and they also
used stacked arcades,
one on top of another,
to construct the great
aqueducts that carried
water to the city.

The Roman aqueduct in Segovia, Spain, uses stacks of arcades to rise high into the air.

THE PONT DU GARD

This aqueduct is called the Pont du Gard.
It is near Nimes, France.
It crosses the Gard River and is much
more massive than the aqueduct
in Segovia.

900 feet long and more than 50 meters high,
the Pont du Gard was begun in 19 B.C.
during the reign of Augustus,
and finished a century later
during the reign of Emperor Trajan.
Trajan ruled from 98 to 117 A.D.

The arch
was strong,
but it also gave
Roman
buildings
grace and
beauty.

Even today,
some of the
Roman ruins
are among
the most
beautiful
designs
in the world.

But the gifts of Rome
to modern civilization
include more than the arch
or Roman architecture.

From the Romans
we also received important ideas
about law and government,
classics of literature,
and perhaps most important,
language.

ROMAN ROCKS,
ROMAN WORDS

Just as many arches that the Romans built
more than 2000 years ago still stand,
so many of the words and parts of words
that the Romans spoke are still spoken.
Even today, we can see familiar words
carved in ancient Roman stones.

LATIN · A BRIDGE TO THE PAST

Latin, the language of the Romans,
is the rock that many modern languages—
including English, Spanish, and others—build on.
In part, English and Spanish are made of Latin,
and so they are a word-bridge to the distant past.

STEMS AND STONES

Just as the Romans put stones
together to make an arch,
so they put parts of words together
to make words.

These word parts, which we call **stems**,
join together to make words.
If we add the stem **pre**,
which means before, to the stem **dict**,
we get the word **predict**.

PRE · DICT
PREDICT

This makes sense! **Pre** means before,
and **dict** means say.
To **predict** is to say something
is going to happen, *before* it does.

Pre is an important stem.
We find the Latin **pre**
in lots of English words, such as **pre**view,
predict, **pre**vent, **pre**school, **pre**cede, **pre**pare,
and even **pre**position.

✎ This is an example to establish the concept of stems. The stem lessons come later.

There are
lots and lots
of Latin stems
like **pre**
that we use
to build words,
both in English
and in other
modern languages,
such as Spanish.

GOOD RELATIVES

By comparing the stems in words
from Latin, English, and Spanish,
we can see that
the two modern languages
are relatives,
which have both descended
from Latin,
their common
ancient source.

LATIN	ENGLISH	SPANISH
praeparare	prepare	preparar
aquaeductus	aqueduct	acueducto
semestris	semester	semestre
semicirculus	semicircular	semicircular
magnanimus	magnanimous	magnánimo
magnitudo	magnitude	magnitud
amphitheatrum	amphitheater	anfiteatro
spectaculum	spectacular	espectaculo
spectrum	specter	espectro
reiterarare	reiterate	reiterar
repetere	repeat	repetir
mediterraneus	mediterranean	mediterráneo
medius	medium	mediano
subterraneus	subterranean	subterráneo

AQUAEDUCTUS
Latin

AQUEDUCT
English

ACUEDUCTO
Spanish

In all three languages,
the stem **aqua** means water,
and **duct** means lead.
The aqueduct led the water to Rome.

Made of arcades of arches,
the aqueducts could cross rivers
and span valleys,
bringing cold, fresh water
down a channel at the top of the aqueduct.

Why did the Romans go to so much trouble to bring water down from the mountains? The Romans did not have pumps, that would let them raise lots of water from underground wells, but they did have gravity, that would move water downhill, from the lakes and rivers high above Rome and their other cities. Sometimes the water was dozens of miles from the city, and the Romans had to build an aqueduct the whole way, creating a gradual slope for miles. The water ran in a channel at the top of the aqueduct, which was lined with lead to prevent leaks. When the engineers came to a steep river valley, they used tiers of arches to raise their aqueduct high into the air. This let the water at the top continue its gentle downhill flow. Today, now that we have underground pipes and large pumps that move water to our cities, we no longer need to build aqueducts, but many of the beautiful aqueducts built by the Romans still stand as a testament to their ancient engineering genius.

GREAT LATIN STEMS

Because Latin stems
are so important to the English language,
we will take a close look
at some of the best stems.

Each one has
its own important meaning.

The stems fit together to make words,
like stones fit together to build an arch.

In the Roman
aqueducts,
the same arch
form was
repeated,
over and
over again.

RE

AGAIN

Re means again.

We find Rome's **re** in English words, we do;
such as **re**peat, **re**turn, **re**verse, **re**view,
revise, **re**flect, **re**call, **re**do,
rehearse, **re**spect, and even **re**new.

When the arches fall to ruin,
we **re**build them, by **re**newing
them again.

Once upon a time,
there was a small stem named Re.
Re saw Sub crouching under an arch,
and Sub said, "Hi!"
"Hi, hi, hi!" said Re.
Sub laughed, in his low voice,
then Re laughed and laughed and laughed.
Sub asked Re,
"Do you remember why
arches are strong, or should I review?"
"I recall," said Re, "I recall."
"Good," said Sub, with new respect.
Then, they looked up
at the keystone.

A RE CLOSEUP

RESPECT

RE ꞏ SPECT

Respect, to admire, is a wonderful word,
containing **re**, again, and **spect**, look.
When we learn to **re**spect someone,
we look at that person again
in a new way!

RE IN SPANISH

Just as **re** is an important stem in English,
it is also important in Spanish.
Here is a Spanish **re** word:

repetir, to repeat

Yo	*quiero*	***re**petir*	*la*	*palabra*.
I	want	to repeat	the	word.

A RE POEM

When Flea saw Skin again,
his feelings were **re**newed.
He stalled, **re**viewed, **re**called
it all, and **re**turned to his food!

See if you can write
a poem of four lines,
using lots of **re** words
and even some rhymes.
It is ok if your poem is funny!

A RE SIMILE

Here is something fun to do.
Pick a **re** word, and then you
compare it to something very different:

A memory IS LIKE a return.

This kind of comparison
is called a simile (SIM ih lee).
Write your own simile and explain it!

An
aqueduct
is
like
respect.

SUB

UNDER

Sub means under.

We find **sub** in English words, to wit:
subtract, **sub**lime, **sub**scribe, **sub**mit,
submarine, and **sub**urb; then we get
substitute, **sub**soil, and **sub**way—they fit!

In **sub**urb's arches, columns stand;
holding up the top, as planned.
Ancient Romans used to toil,
building columns on **sub**soil.

Sub was crawling around, down low,
and here came Re again.
"Ohhhowwww," moaned Sub.
Re started, then stopped, then started,
then stopped. "Sub? Sub?" Re asked.
"Down here," groaned Sub, "Lower."
Re leaned over and peeked
under the lowest arch
and looked again.
"I see you, I see you!" Re said.
"Ohhhh," moaned Sub,
and he burrowed down in the soil,
only his eyes showing.

A SUB CLOSEUP

SUBURB

SUB · URB

Sub means under, and **urb** means city.

A city is an urban place,
but gathered close around
are **sub**urbs where the people live
and travel into town.

SUB IN SPANISH

Just as **sub** is important in English,
it is also important in Spanish.
Here is a Spanish **sub** word:

subyugar, to subjugate
(to subjugate is to conquer or defeat)

Caesar   ***sub****yugó*   *las*   *tribus*   *de Gaul.*
Caesar   subjugated   the   tribes   of Gaul.

A SUB POEM

Sub went underneath the top
of the soil, to help the crop
grow green; down he toiled—
deep in **sub**terranean Roman **sub**soil!

See if you can write
your own poem of four lines,
using lots of **sub** words
and even some rhymes.
It is ok if your poem is funny!

A SUB SIMILE

Let's write another simile,
just to see if we can think cleverly:

A submarine IS LIKE a mole.

Remember, this kind of comparison
is called a simile (SIM ih lee).
Write your own **sub** simile
and explain it.

$$
\begin{array}{r}
4 \\
-\ 1 \\
\hline
3
\end{array}
$$

To
subtract
is like
pulling
one stone
from
an
arch.

DE

DOWN

De means down.

We find **de** in English words, you see,
like **de**scend, **de**posit, and **de**bris,
decay, **de**cide, and then **de**crease,
define, **de**pend, **de**scribe, easy!

When our old buildings **de**cay,
they **de**scend unto the clay,
and there, their **de**bris may stay!

De went down to find Re and Sub.
She leaned down and helped Sub up,
and called for Re. "Re?" she called.
"Here, here here!" cried Re,
and he ran and ran to the spot.
"What's up, Sub?" asked Re,
"You look down. Down. Down."
"Ohhhh," said Sub, "I'm just low."
De looked down at her two buddies.
"Perk up, Sub," she said, and
reached down to pat his back.
"Right, Re?" De asked.
"Right, right. Right," said Re.

A DE CLOSEUP

DESCRIBE

DE · SCRIB

Describe is a **de**scriptive word;
it recalls the moment when we
write, **scrib**, down, **de**, what something is like.
Of course, we don't always write
our **de**scriptions down,
but that is the image in the word!

DE IN SPANISH

Just as **de** is an important stem in English,
it is also important in Spanish.
Here is a Spanish **de** word:

definir, to define

Necesito	**de***finir*	*mis*	*metas*.
I need	to define	my	goals.

A DE POEM

The hawk **de**scended, with good luck,
landing on the aqueduct,
depositing upon the stone,
debris he'd gathered, ere he had flown.

See if you can write
a poem of four lines,
using lots of **de** words
and even some rhymes.
It is ok if your poem is funny!

A DE SIMILE

Now it's time for a simile with de;
do your best, and we will see:

A decrease IS LIKE a leak.

Write your own **de** simile
and explain it!

A
descent
is
like
a
slide.

EX

OUT

Ex means out.

We find **ex** often now, I think:
exit, **ex**tend, **ex**pand, **ex**tinct,
extract, **ex**plode, **ex**pose,
explore, **ex**port, **ex**cept—all those.

If you want the **ex**it, out,
extend your mind, **ex**pand your snout!
Explore the arches, that's the route.

Thinking she was all alone,
Ex looked around,
trying to find the way out.
"Is anybody here?" Ex called.
"Nope," came Sub's voice, from under a rock.
"Not me, not me, not me," came Re's voice,
from somewhere close.
"I'm not here," came De's voice,
in a descending tone.
Then, she saw the arch,
and went through it,
out into the sun.

AN EX CLOSEUP

EXPORT

EX · PORT

Export is a very good word;
to **ex**port a product
is to sell it abroad,
to carry, **port**, it out, **ex**,
of the country.

EX IN SPANISH

Just as **ex** is an **ex**cellent stem in English,
it is also **ex**ceptional in Spanish.
Here is a Spanish **ex** word:

exceder, to define

¿Es		*bueno*	***ex**ceder*	*los*	*límites?*
Is	(it)	good	to exceed	the	limits?

AN EX POEM

These arches, since the day they rose,
have been unto the sun **ex**posed,
Extending up into the air,
to bring fresh water down from there.

See if you can write
a poem of four lines,
using lots of **ex** words,
and even some rhymes.
It is ok if your poem is funny!

AN EX SIMILE

Now it's time for a simile with **ex**;
about an out, as we expect:

An explosion IS LIKE a hooray.

Write your own **ex** simile,
and explain it!

An
extending
column
in an
aqueduct
is like
an
expansive
dream.

SPEC

LOOK

Spec means look.

Of **spec** our language is so full:
in**spec**t, re**spec**t, and **spec**tacle...
spectacular and **spec**trum too,
and **spec**tres haunt Rome's ruins...Boo!

A **spec**tacle is quite a sight,
when gladiators join the fight;
now, Roman **spec**tres haunt the site.
We see 'em in the Coliseum.

Spec looked here,
and spec looked there.
He looked, well, really,
everywhere.
But Ex was out,
and Sub was under,
and Re had done it again—no wonder.
De was down, and wouldn't play,
so Spec just passed the day away,
looking,
we suspect.

A SPEC CLOSEUP

INSPECT

IN · SPEC

Let us inspect this word, *inspect*.
It uses the stem **in**, which means in!
And it also uses **spec**, look.
To in**spec**t is to look into something,
to consider it very carefully.

SPEC IN SPANISH

Spec is an important stem in English,
and it is also part of Spanish.
Here is a Spanish **spec** word:

sospechar, to suspect

Sospecho	*que*	*el*	*hombre*	*tiene*	*muchos*	*libros*.
I suspect	that	the	man	has	many	books.

A SPEC POEM

The **spec**tacles in Roman times
were witnessed by re**spec**tful lines
of Roman **spec**tators who thought
that gladiators bravely fought.

See if you can write
a poem of four lines,
using lots of **spec** words,
and even some rhymes.
It is ok if your poem is funny!

A SPEC SIMILE

Now it's time for a simile with **spec**;
and it should be something to look at:

A spectrum IS LIKE a box of crayons.

Write your own **spec** simile,
and explain it!

Seeing
a
spectacular
view
through
an arch
is like
thinking
hard
about
one
friend.

A STEM STORY

Cold mountain water descended through the channel at the top of the aqueduct, as the architect had repeatedly predicted it would. Unprepared, the people had not believed the architect, when he had described how the aqueduct, with its high arcades of arches, would conduct the water down. Now, thirsty Romans gathered in city squares to inspect the spectacle: fresh water, pouring from spouts. A miracle. Water would not have to be transported. The previously used subterranean wells, with their foul smell, would not be rebuilt. The aqueduct system would be expanded and extended. With ceremony they inscribed the architect's name on a stone. In the distance the spectacular sea rolled, an aquamarine blue, and whitecaps made spots on its surface.

REVIEW

FEATURE STEMS	CLOSEUP WORDS
RE · AGAIN	RESPECT · TO ADMIRE
SUB · UNDER	SUBURB · NEIGHBORHOODS NEAR A CITY
DE · DOWN	DESCRIBE · TO PORTRAY IN WORDS
EX · OUT	EXPORT · TO SELL TO A FOREIGN COUNTRY
SPEC · LOOK	INSPECT · TO EXAMINE SOMETHING

OTHER STEMS WE HAVE NOTICED

STEM	A GOOD EXAMPLE WORD
IN · IN	INSCRIBE · TO WRITE IN
DUCT · LEAD	AQUEDUCT · STRUCTURE THAT BRINGS WATER
PRE · BEFORE	PREDICT · TO SAY SOMETHING WILL HAPPEN

URB · CITY	URBAN · OF THE CITY
DICT · SAY	DICTIONARY · A BOOK ABOUT WORDS
SCRIB · WRITE	SCRIBE · A PERSON WHO WRITES
AQUA · WATER	AQUATIC · OF THE WATER
PORT · CARRY	TRANSPORT · TO MOVE

QUESTIONS TO THINK ABOUT

FOR WHICH STEM CAN YOU THINK OF THE MOST EXAMPLE WORDS?

WHICH EXAMPLE WORD IS MOST LIKE A PICTURE? WHY?

WHICH EXAMPLE WORD MAKES THE MOST SENSE? WHY?

WHICH STEM IS YOUR FAVORITE? WHY?

WHICH NEW WORD ARE YOU LIKELY TO USE? EXPLAIN.

CAN YOU THINK OF YOUR OWN EXAMPLE WORDS FOR THESE STEMS?
WHAT ARE THEY?

SUPER

OVER

Super means over.

A **super**b stem is this one, here;
superior to many, dear.
When **super**stitions cloud your eyes,
this stem will help you realize
how **super**ficial are those ideas!

Roman architects, **super**b,
built their arches, spoke their words,
supervising Roman workers here,
urging them to do **super**ior
work.

Super saw Sub, who was really down.

"Hey, Subby!" giggled Super,

"Isn't this a great day! Wow!"

"You're sure up," groaned Sub.

"Yep, old Subby" beamed Super,

"Where's the gang?"

"O," moaned Sub,

"Re's in his loop,

De's in her slump,

Ex is outa here,

and Spec looks out for himself."

"Not to worry!" cried Super,

"Everything's gonna be all right!"

"Right," said Sub,

and crawled back under the arch.

A SUPER CLOSEUP

SUPERVISE

SUPER · VIS

Supervise is quite a word,
with **super**, over—as you have heard;
and **vis** (like vision), which means look.
(Vis and Spec could write a book.)
To **super**vise is watching over
those who need protection's cover.

SUPER IN SPANISH

Super is an important stem in English,
and it is also part of Spanish.
Here is a Spanish **super** word:

superar, to overcome

Es	*importante*	**super**ar	*nuestros*	*probemas*.
It is	important	to overcome	our	problems.

90

A SUPER POEM

A **super**stitious thing to think
(and **super**ficial) is that drinking
water upside down
makes **super**natural beings frown.

See if you can write
a poem of four lines,
using lots of **super** words,
and even some rhymes.
It is ok if your poem is funny!

A SUPER SIMILE

A simile with **super** must be over-done;
see if you can think of one:

A superstition IS LIKE falling for a trick.

Write your own **super** simile,
and explain it!

The
superior
strength
of the
arch
is like
a
waterfall
in a
photograph.

PRE

BEFORE

Pre means before.

Prepare yourself for this good stem,
it **pre**cedes others, like the limb
precedes the leaves, as you
predict and **pre**view
what comes when, don't you?

The architect had to **pre**dict
the weight of stones—a clever trick;
he then **pre**pared the arches' width,
and **pre**viewed his design, forthwith.

Pre went first and helped Sub
crawl under the arch, down where De was
waiting. Next, Ex came out,
with Spec looking about to make sure
the coast was clear.
Super peeked over the arch,
and Re just did it his own way,
over and over again.
You know him.
Away they went, preceded by Pre,
Ex exiting out, De and Sub
covering the low ground,
Spec looking around,
and Re hopping along behind—
boing, boing, boing.
From here, we lost sight of Pre first.

A PRE CLOSEUP

PRECEDE

PRE · CEDE

Precede means to go before,
with **pre**, before (but there is more).
See, **cede** means go,
and you should know,
that Rome **pre**ceded all we know.

PRE IN SPANISH

Pre is an important stem in English,
and it is also part of Spanish.
Here is a Spanish **pre** word:

preceder, to go before

El	*viento*	**pre***cede*	*a la*	*tormenta.*
The	wind	goes before	the	storm.

A PRE POEM

Roman sages **pre**viewed omens
to **pre**dict their future scares;
Roman citizens were showing
how they **pre**ferred to **pre**pare.

See if you can write
a poem of four lines,
using lots of **pre** words,
and even some rhymes.
It is ok if your poem is funny!

A PRE SIMILE

To make a simile with **pre**,
prepare your idea carefully.

A preview IS LIKE distant thunder.

Write your own **pre** simile,
and explain it!

Predicting
the
future
is like
trying
to see
the
distance.

POST

AFTER

Post means after.

We can't for long **post**pone this stem;
since ***post meridiem*** is called *p.m.*
And as a **post**script we will reason:
P.S.: The games are over by the **post**season.

Our **post**erity come after us,
and carry on our names and such,
we call them our *descendents*, too,
and hope they honor what we do.

The whole gang got organized.
Pre went first, and Post went last.
Sub got on the bottom,
and Super got on the top.
De got down, and Ex went out,
Spec looked all about,
and Re just kept it up and wouldn't quit,
even when they asked him to.
What a kidder.
At the end Post had to make Re stop it.
Re didn't budge.
"Move along," said Post, "After you."
"Okay, okay, okay!" said Re.
Post waited a second
and then followed the others.

A POST CLOSEUP

POSTPONE

POST · PON

Postpone means to put after,
since **post** means after and **pon** means put,
so before you burst into loud laughter,
we've told you what is what!

POST IN SPANISH

Post is an important stem in English,
and it is also part of Spanish.
Here is a Spanish **post** word:

posteridad, posterity
Our posterity are our descendents.

Necesitamos	*pensar*	*en*	*nuestra*	***post*eridad.**
We need	to think	of	our	posterity.

A POST POEM

The pretest is the early check
to see what we don't know;
the **post**test helps us to inspect
if we have learned—Uh oh!

See if you can write
a poem of four lines,
using lots of **post** words,
and even some rhymes.
It is ok if your poem is funny!

A POST SIMILE

Your ideas have to be uncrossed
to make a simile with **post**.

A postscript IS LIKE a small dessert.

Write your own **post** simile,
and explain it!

Our
posterity
are
like
echoes.

PORT

CARRY

Port means carry.

The Romans used to ex**port** loads
trans**port**ing them along the roads,
and im**port** too, with equal ease
to all their Roman colonies.

Barbarians from Gaul (now France)
re**port**ed to their tribes
that Roman legions' **port**able lances
gave them scary vibes!

"Hey, Port," cried Super, "Bring Re over here."
Port picked Re up, but Re cried,
"Put me down, put me down, put me down."
So Port put him down,
on top of Sub, who said
"Ooooff. Get offame, Re,"
and Re rolled onto De, who said
"Hey, get off!" and Re grabbed onto Ex,
who was on her way out, but Ex said,
"Let go, please!" and split, and so Re
bounded toward Post, who was at the back,
but Post said "Yikes! Leave me alone!"
so Re looked at Spec, who had been
watching the whole thing,
but Spec just stared him down.
"Ok," said Re, and Port picked him up again,
and transported him over there.

A PORT CLOSEUP

TRANSPORT

TRANS · PORT

Transport means to move something a distance,
since **trans** means across and **port** means carry;
Julius Caesar trans**port**ed captives, for instance,
back to Rome, which was very
bad luck for them!

PORT IN SPANISH

Port is an important stem in English,
and it is also part of Spanish.
Here is a Spanish **port** word:

portador, carrier

Voy	*a*	*pagar*	*al*	***port**ador*	*de*	*esta*	*carta*.
I'm going		to pay	the	carrier	of	this	letter.

A PORT POEM

Romans had to trans**port** stone
to build the aqueducts,
and **port**ers carried tools alone—
it's re**port**ed in the books!

See if you can write
a poem of four lines,
using lots of **port** words,
and even some rhymes.
It is ok if your poem is funny!

A PORT SIMILE

To make a simile with **port**
you have to be a clever sort.

Transport IS LIKE a leaf on a stream.

Write your own **port** simile,
and explain it!

A
ruin
is like
a
re**port**
from
the
past.

DIS

AWAY

Dis means away.

You will not **dis**agree, we think,
that having a **dis**tracted mind can sink
the best intentions. To **dis**pute this
would be silly; to **dis**miss
it would **dis**tort—or yes—**dis**pose
of truth? Who knows?

The Romans now have **dis**appeared,
and Italy is there,
and Roman arches, as we feared,
are in some **dis**repair.

Dis was trying to sneak away.
He left Post in the back,
and De was too down to notice,
but Spec was watching and saw Dis leave,
as did Super, who had a good view
from over the arch.
Of course, out came Ex,
and Sub warned everyone with his low moan,
from somewhere under the arch.
Pre came after Dis first,
and Port hurried along, carrying Re,
whose "Stop it, stop it, stop it"
repeated across the fields.
They were too late.
Slowly, Dis made it.
He disappeared.

A DIS CLOSEUP

DISTRACT

DIS · TRACT

To be **distracted**, as you know,
is to lose your attention, yes, in full;
for **dis** means away, and **tract** means pull—
but we're too **dis**tracted to listen now.

DIS IN SPANISH

Dis is an important stem in English,
and it is also part of Spanish.
Here is a Spanish **dis** word:

distancia, distance

Yo	*veo*	*la*	*ciudad*	*en*	*la*	***dis**tancia.*
I	see	the	city	in	the	distance.

A DIS POEM

Though Rome has **dis**appeared today,
its words have been **dis**persed.
Like **dis**tant poems that we say,
distributed in verse.

See if you can write
a poem of four lines,
using lots of **dis** words,
and even some rhymes.
It is ok if your poem is funny!

A DIS SIMILE

To make a simile with **dis**
—don't **dis**agree—it looks like this:

An arch in a ruin IS LIKE a distant sound.

Write your own **dis** simile,
and explain it!

Long
shadows
are like
distracted
minds.

REVIEW
FEATURED LATIN STEMS

DE · DOWN

EX · OUT

RE · AGAIN

SPEC · LOOK

SUB · UNDER

SUPER · OVER

PRE · BEFORE

POST · AFTER

PORT · CARRY

DIS · AWAY

OTHER STEMS WE HAVE NOTICED

STEM	A GOOD EXAMPLE WORD
IN · IN	INSCRIBE · TO WRITE IN
DUCT · LEAD	AQUEDUCT · STRUCTURE THAT BRINGS WATER
URB · CITY	URBAN · OF THE CITY
DICT · SAY	DICTIONARY · A BOOK ABOUT WORDS
SCRIB · WRITE	SCRIBE · A PERSON WHO WRITES
AQUA · WATER	AQUATIC · OF THE WATER
VIS - LOOK	VISION - THE SENSE OF SIGHT
CEDE - GO	PRECEDE - TO GO BEFORE
PON - PUT	POSTPONE - TO DELAY
TRANS - ACROSS	TRANSPORT - TO MOVE SOMETHING A DISTANCE
TRACT - PULL	DISTRACT - TO HAVE YOUR ATTENTION PULLED AWAY

THE SECRET OF WORDS

Now that we have learned important Latin stems, let's think about what we know. The English we speak is not new; it is a modern descendent of ancient Latin, and is a close relative of Spanish, which is even more similar to Latin. English and Spanish share many things, so to learn either is to learn some of the other. Both languages give modern voice to the ancient Romans, who conquered most of the Mediterranean world more than 2,000 years ago. One of Rome's gifts to civilization is the Roman arch that has been important to architecture ever since.

Like stones in the arch, Latin stems combine to make many English words. The stems we have learned are only a beginning. There are many more. Each stem is part of dozens or even hundreds of English and Spanish words, and by knowing the stem, you now know a part of the meaning of the word and why the word is spelled the way it is. Stems make vocabulary easy, powerful, and fun. By learning these Latin stems, you have begun to understand who you are, and where important parts of your mind came from.